CROCODILES

— BUILT FOR THE HUNT —

by Tammy Gagne

Consultant: Dr. Jackie Gai, DVM
Wildlife Veterinarian

CAPSTONE PRESS
a capstone imprint

First Facts are published by Capstone Press,
1710 Roe Crest Drive, North Mankato, Minnesota 56003
www.capstonepub.com

Library of Congress Cataloging-in-Publication Data
Cataloging-in-Publication Data is on file with the Library of Congress.
ISBN 978-1-4914-5038-3 (library binding)
ISBN 978-1-4914-5082-6 (eBook PDF)

Editorial Credits
Brenda Haugen, editor; Juliette Peters, designer; Tracy Cummins,
media researcher; Katy LaVigne, production specialist

Photo Credits
Getty Images: Cultura RM/Lou Coetzer, 5, DEA/C.DANI-I.JESKE, 7, Federico Veronesi,
20, Ian Waldie, 6, Mike Korostelev, 18, Peter Walton Photography, 1, Sylvain Cordier, 19,
Victoria Stone & Mark Deeble, 10; iStockphoto: Byronsdad, 8; Shutterstock: alexnika, 12,
apiguide, 15, Audrey Snider-Bell, Cover, dangdumrong, 16, Ian Scott, 11, Back Cover,
Johan Swanepoel, 3, konmesa, 2, 17, Mogens Trolle, 13, Nila Newsom, 21, pashabo,
Design Element, Stuart G Porter, 9.

Printed in China by Nordica
0415/CA21500544
042015   008845NORDF15

TABLE OF CONTENTS

OUT OF NOWHERE

A zebra strolls toward a river for a drink. A hungry crocodile waits in the water. When the zebra lowers its head, the powerful **predator** springs into action. The crocodile grabs its helpless **prey**.

Crocodiles are deadly predators. They hunt many kinds of prey, including small **mammals**, fish, deer, and birds.

FACT

Crocodiles also hunt some very large animals. They can even kill a small hippopotamus that weighs about 5,000 pounds (2,268 kilograms). That's bigger than an average car!

predator—an animal that hunts other animals for food

prey—an animal hunted by another animal for food

mammal—a warm-blooded animal that breathes air; mammals have hair or fur; female mammals feed milk to their young

BIG AND STRONG

Saltwater crocodiles are the largest crocodiles. They can grow up to 22 feet (6.7 meters) long. This **species** uses its size and strength to overpower prey.

Nile crocodiles are smaller but still big and strong. They grow to about 16 feet (5 m) long. Like saltwater crocodiles, Nile crocodiles use their size and power for hunting. But Nile crocodiles will also eat dead animals left by other predators.

FACT

A saltwater crocodile has the strongest bite in the animal kingdom. It can crush the skull of a fully-grown water buffalo.

species—a group of animals with similar features

ATTACK!

Crocodiles can run faster than people do. But they do not waste energy chasing prey on land. Crocodiles wait for prey to come to them. As soon as a prey animal moves within reach, a crocodile **lunges** at it. Moving through water takes less energy. Crocodiles often swim after fish and turtles.

FACT

Some crocodiles have thin **snouts** that can grab prey from underwater holes. Their snouts act like giant tweezers to nab small prey such as shrimp.

lunge—to move forward quickly and suddenly

snout—a long front part of an animal's head; the snout includes the nose, mouth, and jaws

A FAST SWIMMER

Crocodiles move fast when chasing prey in the water. The Nile crocodile can swim 18 miles (29 kilometers) per hour. That is about three times faster than an Olympic swimmer!

A crocodile can hold its breath a long time. A crocodile waiting for prey can stay underwater up to two hours.

GRAB AND DRAG

Crocodiles have 60 to 75 razor-sharp teeth. They use their teeth for catching and holding onto prey. After getting a firm grip on prey, crocodiles drag their prey underwater and drown it.

FACT

When a crocodile loses a tooth, another tooth grows in its place. A crocodile may have 3,000 teeth in its lifetime!

SHARP SENSES

Crocodiles have sharp senses to help them hunt. They can see well both on land and in the water. They also have excellent hearing. Crocodiles can hear many sounds that humans cannot. Crocodiles have large **lobes** in their brains that help them smell nearby animals.

lobe—a curved or rounded part of an organ, such as the brain

A THICK SKIN

Tough scales called **scutes** cover most of a crocodile's body. These bony scales act like a suit of armor. Even if prey tries to bite back, a crocodile will almost always win the battle.

FACT

Crocodiles are always growing new scutes. As new scutes move into place, the old ones fall out.

scute—a wide scale

BY LEAPS AND BOUNDS

Crocodiles are skilled jumpers. They can leap several feet into the air. They use their strong tails to push themselves into the air. Many crocodiles catch birds this way.

EVENING MEALS

Crocodiles are **nocturnal**. They do most of their hunting at night. Crocodiles often sleep in the daytime sun. But they are always on alert. A crocodile can go from snoozing to snapping in just seconds.

nocturnal—active at night and resting during the day

AMAZING BUT TRUE!

Crocodiles can go without food for a long time. Most crocodiles eat only about 50 times each year. Crocodiles can survive an entire year without eating anything at all!

GLOSSARY

lobe (LOHB)—a curved or rounded part of an organ, such as the brain

lunge (LUHNJ)—to move forward quickly and suddenly

mammal (MAM-uhl)—a warm-blooded animal that breathes air; mammals have hair or fur; female mammals feed milk to their young

nocturnal (nok-TUR-nuhl)—active at night and resting during the day

predator (PRED-uh-tur)—an animal that hunts other animals for food

prey (PRAY)—an animal hunted by another animal for food

scute (SKOOT)—a wide scale

snout (SNOUT)—a long front part of an animal's head; the snout includes the nose, mouth, and jaws

species (SPEE-sheez)—a group of animals with similar features

READ MORE

Barr, Brady. *Crocodile Encounters: And More True Stories of Adventures with Animals.* Washington, D.C.: National Geographic, 2012.

Hamilton, Sue. *Attacked by a Crocodile.* Close Encounters of the Wild Kind. Edina, Minn.: ABDO, 2010.

Niver, Heather Moore. *20 Fun Facts About Crocodiles.* New York: Gareth Stevens Pub., 2012.

INTERNET SITES

FactHound offers a safe, fun way to find Internet sites related to this book. All of the sites on FactHound have been researched by our staff.

Here's all you do:

Visit *www.facthound.com*

Type in this code: 9781491450383

Super-cool stuff!

Check out projects, games and lots more at
www.capstonekids.com

CRITICAL THINKING USING THE COMMON CORE

1. Does a crocodile's body help protect it during a fight? How? (Key Ideas and Details)

2. Look at the Fact box on page 8. In what other ways might a long, thin snout be useful to a crocodile? (Craft and Structure)

INDEX